YOU ONLY LIVE TWICE

HANNAH MULDOON

YOU ONLY LIVE TWICE

When Inner Strength Is All You Have

HANNAH MULDOON

You Only Live Twice
Copyright © 2023 Hannah Muldoon
First published in 2023

Print: 978-1-76124-123-9
E-book: 978-1-76124-124-6

All rights reserved. No part of this book may be reproduced, stored in a retrieval system, or transmitted by any means (electronic, mechanical, photocopying, recording, or otherwise) without written permission from the author.

Because of the dynamic nature of the Internet, any web addresses or links contained in this book may have changed since publication and may no longer be valid. The information in this book is based on the author's experiences and opinions. The views expressed in this book are solely those of the author and do not necessarily reflect the views of the publisher; the publisher hereby disclaims any responsibility for them.

The author of this book does not dispense any form of medical, legal, financial, or technical advice either directly or indirectly. The intent of the author is solely to provide information of a general nature to help you in your quest for personal development and growth. In the event you use any of the information in this book, the author and the publisher assume no responsibility for your actions. If any form of expert assistance is required, the services of a competent professional should be sought.

Photographer for cover image: Aya Chatila

Publishing information
Publishing and design facilitated by Passionpreneur Publishing
A division of Passionpreneur Organization Pty Ltd
ABN: 48640637529

Melbourne, VIC | Australia
www.PassionpreneurPublishing.com

*This book is dedicated to my mum, Linda.
You are the best!
You held my hand, and never let go.
You never gave up even when the light at the end of the tunnel felt as if it was getting further away.*

TABLE OF CONTENTS

Acknowledgements   ix

Chapter 1
LONDON TRIP
"One week of vacation almost costs me my life."   1

Chapter 2
SLEEPING BEAUTY
"Definitely not a fairytale"   15

Chapter 3
RECOVERY
"Trying to find ways not to give up"   35

Chapter 4
GETTING BACK TO "NORMAL"
"Taking my life back"   53

Chapter 5
WHEN WILL IT BE OVER?
"Is there a light at the end of the tunnel?"   63

ACKNOWLEDGEMENTS

I would like to acknowledge my family - my mum, my dad and my brother - for dropping everything so they could be by my side and support me for months.

I would like to thank all my friends for being there for me and loving me unconditionally. To India for being the greatest friend I could ever ask for. To my friend Izzy for always making me smile even on the darkest day. And to my friend Hannan for showing me how to have fun and live my life again. I am extremely grateful to all of my friends for making me who I am today. Also to Harvey, I am so grateful for you and your ability to make me forget all my worries and for making me the happiest version of myself.

I would also like to express my gratitude to Maria, my Careers coach and friend. You never doubted me for a second and always saw the best in me.

Thank you for never giving up on me. To all the staff at DESC, Andy and Fiona for welcoming me back to school and checking on me every chance you could get. To Maggie for helping my family and for your kindness.

Finally to Jill and Sarah, thank you for saving my life and taking me to the hospital when we were in London. I am forever grateful to you.

CHAPTER 1
LONDON TRIP

"One week of vacation almost costs me my life."

SEPTEMBER 2019

My future was so unclear when I was 15. I had absolutely no idea where I was going to end up. But I was obviously not expecting what happened to me. I don't want to write about this chapter of my life. I just want to move on. I don't want to keep reliving this story, having spent so long trying to forget these events. Maybe if I don't think about it, I'll forget it. Is that even possible?

This was a huge event in my life and I had to live through it. I am still living it. Why did I go on the school trip? I never really wanted to go. I was not a fan of the UK and wasn't even interested in the planned activities! If I hadn't gone, maybe my life would be different today. I felt like I just keep making mistake after mistake. What if I had changed one thing, would it have made a difference? I feel like if I was to go through something similar now, the outcome would be different.

I hate that I can't go back and change it. It makes me angry that my actions had permanent consequences. I was only 15 at the time and was so unaware of how dangerous life could be. I never would have thought a school trip could go so wrong. I can't believe that I am still suffering the consequences. I still haven't healed fully, and I still need physiotherapy, even after 3 years.

The story starts at the beginning of the school year when I was in year 11. I had just turned 15. One of my best and only friends had just moved back home to Canada. I never got to say a proper goodbye to her, but I figured that I would see her during one of the school holidays.

At the beginning of the school year, some time in September of 2019, my music teacher told us about a school trip to London with the performing arts department. Initially, I did not want to go at all. To be honest, I hated the idea of going. My favourite places to visit in the UK are the airports, so that I can leave! And I was just not interested in the activities I was going to have to take part in. To be honest, it was literally my worst nightmare.

I was quite shy at the time, and I was never into acting or dancing. I hated performing in front of people. It wasn't until my music teacher told us that, if we went on the trip, we would miss an entire week of school that I became more interested in going. I didn't hesitate after she told us this. Sign me up! I was having trouble with one of my teachers, who I felt didn't like me, and I felt like I just really needed to escape him for a week.

I was always finding ways to skip school. I hated it so much. I wasn't doing well mentally, as I had lost someone close to me a couple of months before: my grandad. I didn't really know how to handle the passing of a family member. I had never lost someone so close to me before and, to be honest, I never really got over it. I was never the same because of it. I had left school early the summer before to visit him, which was one of the last times I saw him. I didn't tell many people about it, though. The teacher who didn't like me felt the need to call me out in front of everyone for missing the last few weeks of Year 10. He loved making jokes about me, even when I wasn't there. He must have really liked me because he was ALWAYS talking about me.

The passing of my grandad hit me hard, as it would for anyone. We were really close, not just because I was most definitely his favourite member of the family and favourite grandchild, but because he was always there for me. He never needed me to have an illness to show that he loved me. He and my granny would always be the first to call on my birthday and they would always come and visit us in Dubai. Not just because in Dubai we were free accommodation (so they didn't have to pay for a hotel), but because they really wanted to see us. Watching him battle cancer for 18 months was draining. The way he changed over time physically, emotionally, and mentally, was tough.

Not having him around anymore was a lot harder than I could ever have imagined. I struggled to go to school, which led to me being sent to the guidance counsellor every week. I didn't really mind because she was really nice and seemed kind of like a friend (but not really at all). I never told the group of friends I sat with at lunch at the time as I was embarrassed. We were never close friends so they never really noticed when I went missing once a week. But my best friend India eventually figured it out. She was always very intelligent and could read me like a book. Also, I do confess that I would use the counsellor as an excuse to skip the lessons where I would have to see the evil teacher … And I'd do it again if I had to!

NOVEMBER 2019

A week before the trip, I started to feel ill with flu-like symptoms and had to stay home from school. I didn't think anything of it. This happened maybe once a year, as it does to everyone. Of course, I just assumed that I would be back at school after I got better so I never got to say a proper goodbye to my friends. I don't remember our last interactions. The first day I remember feeling sick was the 9th of November. I was at a water park with my cousin that day. Going to water parks was one of my favourite things to do, I never thought that it would be the last time I would go there.

My mum wanted me to see a doctor to make sure I was well enough to go on the trip because, as the days passed, I still wasn't getting better. This doctor tested me for influenza, but the test came back negative. She assured my mum and I that I did not have influenza and that I could go on the school trip, and she gave me some medicine to take with me in case I started to feel unwell again. I felt as if I was crazy because this *super amazing* doctor told me that I just had a cold. It must have been a very strong cold if I couldn't even get out of bed. The medicine she prescribed me was an antibiotic used to treat bacterial infections and I was later on told that this would not have treated influenza at all and was basically useless.

I never went back to school after that. I don't even remember my last day of year 11. I was so miserable at school back then, but I would do anything now to go back in time, even if it was just for one day. You never truly appreciate something until it's gone. On the day of my flight, I was dreading going. I was not excited at all. I couldn't believe that these were the lengths I was going to in order to escape one teacher. I packed 20 minutes before I had to leave for my flight. Even then, my mum did most of it. I felt extremely guilty for not being excited to go, because my mum had paid a lot of money for me to go on this school trip. I just really needed to escape.

Originally, the school nurse wasn't meant to go on the trip to London, but there was another student on the trip who had a medical condition. I don't think this student even ended up going on the trip in the end, but whoever they were, they played a big part in saving my life. I have no idea how differently things would have turned out if not for them. My mum had told Nurse Jill that I had been sick earlier that week, and from then on she made sure to look out for me.

All I remember from being at the airport that day was feeling too sick to eat anything. When we got on the plane, almost everyone fell asleep. Of course, I wasn't able to sleep and I stayed awake for the whole 7-hour plane journey. The first few days in London I absolutely hated. I didn't like any of the activities we had to do, which involved things like dancing which made me extremely uncomfortable. There weren't many musical activities, which I would have enjoyed a lot more. I don't know if it was just because I was sick, but the food seemed to make me feel worse every time I ate, like I wanted to throw up. Later, when I felt a little bit better, I enjoyed the shows we attended. I had never been to a West End show in London.

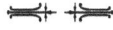

15TH OF NOVEMBER 2019

On Friday the 15th of November we got to do some independent sightseeing in London. People were able to go and meet up with friends and family. As I didn't have any friends in London and all my family lived in Scotland, I tagged along with my friends and had lunch with them and their families.

After we all had lunch and did a little bit of shopping in the city, we went to a history experience exhibition where we learned about wars and specific historical events. It contained live actors, virtual reality and interactive scenes. It felt almost like a haunted house to walk through. I remember feeling fine going in and I thought I might finally be getting better. But walking through the history experience, I knew something was wrong. There were smoke machines everywhere, and we were all breathing in the smoke. It was dry and had a strange smell, and it made me feel uncomfortable. A few other people commented on it, too. Once my group had finished in the exhibition we waited for the others outside. I remember feeling that my throat was aching. I had never felt that much pain in my throat before. I went into the dirty London bathroom because I felt ill, as if I was about to vomit. I stood by the toilet in the dark bathroom but nothing happened. I decided maybe it was a false alarm and that maybe I was just being dramatic about the smoke machine.

Once all the groups had finished their experience, it was time to go for dinner. I remember approaching the school nurse on the way to the restaurant and telling her I wasn't feeling well. She told me that if I had any problems, I had to go and see her. I always hesitated when speaking to her because I hated feeling like a burden. I kept thinking, "Maybe I'm just being dramatic, maybe there's nothing wrong with me". The last thing I wanted was to keep bothering her: this was her trip as well. At some point on the bus trip, I remember crying to my friend because I started to feel so sick. She kept offering to get the nurse, but I kept reassuring her that I was fine.

Once we got to the Italian restaurant, we all went to the downstairs seating area where there was space for the whole group. I couldn't eat any of my food when it arrived. I tried to eat, but I felt like there was something wrong. My friends had worried expressions on their faces, but they didn't really know what to do either. I decided to go upstairs to the bathroom because I felt again that I might throw up. I spent a long time in there, crying in a bathroom stall, and I even tried to make myself sick, but nothing worked. A few students were coming in and out of the bathroom, many asking if I was ok. One of my friends came in and asked what was wrong. "I'm fine, I'm just dying", I joked to her. I didn't want to worry her.

I began to feel more frustrated and began crying again. Another girl came into the bathroom once my friend had left and asked me if I was ok. I decided enough was enough and I asked if she could get a teacher. Once the teacher came in, I asked if she could get the nurse for me because I needed to do something about this. I was tired of crying in bathrooms and constantly feeling sick.

She brought me to a table upstairs in the empty part of the restaurant and she gave me a glass of water. I explained to her what was happening and how I felt and she immediately ran down to the nearest pharmacy to get me some medicine. I was so grateful for her help, but felt bad that I had made her go out instead of letting her eat dinner with the rest of the teachers. What if I was just wasting her time?

The bus ride back to the hotel we were staying at is hard to remember, apart from me crying on my friend's shoulder and still feeling awful. The bus was so loud, which made everything worse. I vaguely remember the nurse telling me that if I had any problems in the night or I wasn't feeling well, I had to go see her. Of course, I didn't think that would be necessary. I got into the room and went straight to bed, without talking to anyone. I tried so hard to fall asleep that night but I kept coughing constantly. The older girls in the room were still awake and kept asking if I was ok. I reassured them that I was fine but as time went on, one of them reminded me of what Nurse Jill had said to do if I was unwell. I was hesitant at first, but I felt guilty that my coughing was disturbing the other girls who were just trying to sleep.

16TH OF NOVEMBER 2019, 1:00 AM

The older girl asked me if I needed her to come with me. At first I said no, but when I went out into the hallway, I couldn't find the nurse's room. It was the strangest feeling. Why had I suddenly forgotten which room she was in? I looked down the hallway and couldn't figure it out. What was happening to me? I went back to ask for one of the older girls' help, and she took me to the door and then went back to the room. I knocked on the door. Right when I pulled my hand back from the door, I started not being able to breathe. I was gasping for air, but no oxygen seemed to be getting to my lungs. I remember trying to sit down on the floor to try and calm myself down and catch my breath but I ended up falling to the ground. I had my hand on my chest and my eyes closed as I tried to breathe. I don't remember who opened the door, but I said something along the lines of, "Help, I can't breathe".

The nurse sat on the floor next to me and felt my pulse as the drama teacher she was sharing a room with stood by the door. She knew something was wrong with me and told me that I needed to go to hospital right away. While sitting on the floor, I managed to catch my breath a little bit. They told me to get changed into some clothes, so I went back to my room. The older girl who had taken me to Nurse Jill's door was still awake, so I told her that I was going to the hospital. I tried to laugh about it, so as not to scare her. I quickly changed and I took my bag with me, just in case I needed it.

We sat on comfy red leather seats in the lobby of the hotel as we waited for the taxi. Once we finally got in the taxi, we asked to be taken to the nearest hospital. I think Nurse Jill was comforting me and holding me, knowing I was scared. The driver took us to the Chelsea and Westminster Hospital. When we got inside the Accident and Emergency Department, I sat down in the waiting room. Because I wasn't a resident in the UK and I wasn't with my parents, the process was a lot more difficult than we would have liked it to be. They kept asking me questions and my mind was so all over the place that I struggled to answer. I was having trouble remembering anything. For example, my family had just moved house and I completely forgot my new address. We had to fill out a lot of forms, and just when I thought we had completed them, more forms were brought to us. I could see that Nurse Jill was frustrated that they were not letting me see a doctor. Finally, I was taken into a room where a nurse took my vitals. This doctor came in and told me my vitals were normal and everything was fine. I remember feeling so guilty for dragging the school nurse and drama teacher to a hospital in the middle of the night.

However, the school nurse wasn't convinced. She didn't want to take me back to the hotel when I couldn't breathe. They took me into a different room where I lay on the bed. At this point, no one was telling me anything. I was so confused. The nurse at the hospital was trying different oxygen masks on me but I kept pulling them off because I told her I couldn't breathe in any of them, and I felt as if I was going to be sick. The memory is very blurry now, but I remember crying a lot.

I remember asking them to hold my hair back because I was going to vomit and, of course, I didn't want to get anything in my silky hair. It's my best feature! They were trying to get hold of my parents but it was the middle of the night for my dad, who was in Manchester at the time. As for my mum in Dubai, it was too early in the morning for her to answer. They finally managed to get hold of my mum on the phone, and the nurse handed it to me so I could speak to her. All I remember saying to her on the phone was something along the lines of, "I miss you, I want to go home". I gave the phone back to the nurse. All I wanted was my mum at this point. I'll never forget the last thing I remember seeing, which was the teacher's face. She looked scared but as if she was trying not to show it in front of me, hiding her fear behind a smile. That was the last thing I remember. Apparently, after this I began to cough up blood. I don't remember that at all. But that seems like a pretty hard thing to forget …

CHAPTER 2
SLEEPING BEAUTY

"Definitely not a fairytale"

16TH OF NOVEMBER 2019

When my mum was on the phone with me at around 3:30 am London time, she could barely understand me. She said that she thought I was already delirious and that the toxins of the bacteria were taking over my body. Once we hung up the phone, she called my dad who was in Manchester with my brother. She told him that he needed to drive to London and get to me as fast as possible. My mum packed a bag of clothes and got on the next flight, 4 hours after our phone call. At the time, she didn't know how serious my condition was because the teachers didn't want to scare her. However, she still got on a flight, just to be with me. My dad had then called my aunt who lived in London to go to the hospital. She arrived at 9 am, but she wasn't allowed to see me. My dad arrived at 12:34 pm. He wasn't allowed to see me for 20 minutes as, by that time, there were many doctors trying to save my life.

At about 1 pm, they let my dad and aunt in but they only pulled the curtain back to let them see me from afar. There were around 13 doctors at the bed and one doctor was manually pumping the heart machine to keep me alive. I wasn't supposed to be connected to a heart machine. However, when they tried to connect me to the extracorporeal membrane oxygenation (ECMO) machine, which provides respiratory support, they ended up inserting the cannula, the tube, into my artery instead of my veins. The job of the ECMO is to pump blood outside the body to a heart-lung machine that removes carbon dioxide and sends oxygen-filled blood back to tissues in the body. An ECMO is used in critical care situations when the heart and lungs need to heal.

My parents believe this incident is what caused me to have a cardiac arrest which resulted in heart problems. I then proceeded to need the ECMO machine's support. When the medical staff inserted the cannula in my artery, a doctor tried to pull it out, but it snapped off. They couldn't remove it then and there because I was having a heart attack and wouldn't have survived.

My mum had had a long 7-hour flight, during which she cried nonstop. She arrived at the hospital around 5 pm. It's all a bit of a blur for anyone to remember. My mum remembers my dad crying and the doctors coming to tell them that I had been operated on to be connected to the ECMO machine to clean my blood and that I had to be transferred to the Royal Brompton Hospital. The doctors said that the next 24 hours were critical.

17TH OF NOVEMBER 2019

My family all slept in the hospital waiting room that night, waiting patiently to hear from the doctors to make sure I was okay. At this point I had many family members dropping everything and just coming straight down to London to see me, most of whom were coming from Scotland. My brother took a train from Manchester without, of course, being told of the severity of the situation. Eventually, I almost had my entire family in that waiting room: 3 of my uncles, 2 aunts, my cousin, my granny and of course my mum, dad and brother. My aunt and uncle who lived in London took my brother and granny to stay in their house.

The doctor came out to see my parents and told them that he was very worried about my condition but he was encouraged by the fact that I hadn't gotten any worse. He was happy that I had been stabilised in the condition I was in. He also confirmed that they knew I had a certain strain of influenza type A/H3N2 and also a certain strain of Staphylococcus aureus PVL-SA. Staphylococcus aureus is a bacteria, but the PVL strain is a toxin produced by certain types of staphylococcus aureus which kills white blood cells and causes damage to the skin and deeper tissue. Even the doctors were confused about how I caught this illness. At this point I was put on a ventilator to help me breathe, plus the ECMO machine, and a machine to pump my heart. The doctor also told my parents that they were preparing for my kidneys to fail so they were getting the kidney dialysis machine ready.

The hospital gave them beds to sleep in that day so they got better sleep. All my friends from the trip were asking to come visit me as they missed me but were also confused by my absence and couldn't understand why I wasn't answering my phone. The school didn't tell any of the students that I was in a coma until everyone got back from the London trip, as they didn't want to worry or scare anyone. So my friends just thought I was sitting in bed eating ice cream and pizza. Unfortunately, I was not ...

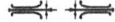

18TH OF NOVEMBER 2019

As the doctors had predicted, my kidneys had failed completely. So I was hooked up to the dialysis machine, which is just what I needed. More tubes in my body … I was actually on this machine for a while as the kidneys can be quite lazy to wake up again. Doctors feared that I might be on this machine for the rest of my life. I absolutely hated it when I eventually woke up. It was basically 2 tubes in my chest. One was taking out the blood from my body and filtering it through the machine to clean it. The other tube returned the blood to my body. However, the machine and tubes made the blood so cold when it returned back through me. They had a heater on the returning tube to try and warm the blood up but it still made me freeze. I was always shivering.

I was receiving so much fluid through drips that my whole body was swollen. Although this fluid was normal for an ICU patient to try and stabilise them, it was really distressing for my mum to see. Every part of my body had swollen up to the point where I didn't even look like myself. I always tell my mum how I wish she had taken a picture of me just to see what I looked like, but she made sure no one took any pictures as she never wanted me to see the way I looked at the time.

The doctors were encouraged by the work my heart had done, circulating blood to the lower limbs. There was a reverse of toxins in my right leg and my left leg seemed to be more balanced.

19TH OF NOVEMBER 2019

The doctors were saying that I was still pretty sick and every 24 hours was critical for my recovery. My parents were just glad that I had made it through the night. They, along with my brother, had to go see the psychologist in the hospital. This really changed my mum's perspective. She willed me to get better every day, and she never left my side. She would sing to me, play my favourite music (although sometimes she would sneak some of her favourite songs on), read letters from my friends and just hold my hand. The psychologist told her that I was probably going to be really scared when I woke up, much like I was when I was last awake on the 16th of November. She told my mum that she needed to be strong for me, as did everyone. My mum made sure that I was going to get better and made sure to check up with every doctor she could every day. I'm convinced that she thinks that she actually is a doctor herself. From this day on, my mum also started writing in a diary every day, so I could read back on all the days I missed from being in the coma.

20TH OF NOVEMBER 2019

The school nurse and the drama teacher came in to say goodbye. They came in daily to check up on me but the school trip was over and everyone had to go back to Dubai now. My friends on the school trip and in Dubai still had no idea what had happened because the school didn't want to worry the kids on the trip and just wanted to get them home safely. But eventually, when everyone got back, they had an assembly about me to explain the situation. (I was honoured. A whole assembly about me? You shouldn't have).

The doctors were very worried about my left leg and were thinking about opening up the calf to let the muscle breathe. It's called compartment syndrome, which occurs when the pressure inside a muscle increases, restricting the blood flow to the area which can potentially damage the muscles and nearby nerves and cause pain. Fortunately, I was in a coma and I do not remember feeling the pain. However, the doctors didn't think I was strong enough for another operation so they let me rest more.

21ST OF NOVEMBER 2019

On this day I was fed some nutrients through a drip to try to help me progress. My lungs were still full of fluid. They reduced some of the paralysis drugs at 11 am to test my brain activity. The doctor said there were so many toxins in my body and I needed more time to recover.

My mum was still playing some music to try to relax me and was always holding my hand! My aunt had brought me a book that she read to me. All the love and support from everyone really helped my parents and my brother keep strong.

22ND OF NOVEMBER 2019

At 11 pm, my parents got a call from the doctors saying that they needed to go to the hospital for a meeting. They were terrified. Once they got back to the hospital they met with two doctors. The doctors told my parents that I had fluid outside my lungs which was infected and had to be treated before it moved around my body. They were worried about my leg and how the poison from the dead cells going around my body may result in having to amputate my left leg to save my life. They had to agree and sign that it was okay for them to do this surgery if necessary. My mum felt physically sick and just cried. She would rub my legs all the time because she wanted so badly for them to heal. She would call it "mummy magic". It seemed to be a great tactic because I still have my legs!

My parents walked back to the residence like zombies, but when they got there, there were fire engines. Apparently, there was a burst pipe and the whole place was flooded. They wouldn't let them in but my mum made my dad go in and get her phone and the bags. As they dragged their suitcases in the pouring rain, one of the wheels fell off a suitcase. They both looked at each other in disbelief at how many things were going wrong that night. They ended up back at the hospital and one of the nurses who often looked after me found them. They ended up sleeping in an empty kids' ward.

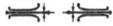

23RD OF NOVEMBER 2019

My parents woke up that morning relieved not to have received another call from the hospital. They rushed to see me and saw that I was okay with my leg still intact. The doctors had decided not to do anything about my lungs. They wanted to watch my leg and make sure it was okay and to observe what was happening. They found a pulse in my left ankle, which was a positive sign, and found that blood was flowing to the foot. The swelling in my leg was going down.

This was the first day I squeezed my mum's hand, apparently, which made her so happy. Although, one of her friends came to visit her and the first thing he said to my mum was, "you look like shit". It made her laugh though.

25TH OF NOVEMBER 2019

The doctor in charge that day told my parents that my lung had collapsed due to the amount of fluid and air outside my lungs. She told them that they would need to insert a drain to my lungs to drain the fluid as it was too dangerous to leave. (It left me with a cool scar which I tell everyone was a bullet wound). This was a scary procedure for my parents as it was something the hospital had been putting off for days, saying that it was too dangerous and there would be a high risk of bleeding as I was on blood thinners for the ECMO machine. The doctors even made them sign a consent form to allow the doctors to do the procedure. However, the procedure ended up going well and 1.5 litres of fluid was removed.

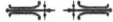

27TH OF NOVEMBER 2019

The doctors discovered that the line draining the fluid and air from my lungs wasn't working properly and air was building up, causing my lungs to collapse again. The small drain was immediately removed and replaced with a larger one. Apparently, there was a large "pop" and all the air escaped at once. Unfortunately, when the larger drain was inserted, it made the ECMO machine stop working. So, immediately, all the doctors had to intervene. They had to insert new leads into my neck for more drugs to be administered, and when they did this, they couldn't stop the bleeding. Eventually, everything calmed down and they managed to stabilise me.

1ST OF DECEMBER 2019

My aunt had brought a Christmas advent calendar from her work which my mum would open every day in December. Each day she would video herself opening it with someone so I could see what was in each day. My mum wanted to make sure I didn't miss a single day. And eventually, all the nurses and even some doctors were fighting over who got to be in the next advent calendar video. They are very funny to look back on. My mum and aunt opened the first one, and inside it was a sparkly pink lip gloss! My brother just watched and laughed at them.

20TH OF DECEMBER 2019

When I woke up, it wasn't a "Sleeping Beauty" moment. My eyes didn't suddenly open, and I didn't suddenly sit up and say "hello" to everyone again. I didn't have a Prince Charming waiting for me. I don't really remember the exact moment I woke up. I had a lot of terrifying nightmares when I was in the coma, where I was just dying over and over again. So when I woke up, I didn't know it was real.

The days that followed my waking up were slow and frustrating for my family. I kept drifting in and out of consciousness. I couldn't stay awake for long as I was heavily medicated. I remember very little of my time in ICU, and some of my memories were traumatising. I experienced a lot of delirium due to the amount of sleep deprivation, because when you're in a medically induced coma, you're not actually sleeping, just unconscious. So, I hadn't slept properly in 6 weeks. I was hallucinating some crazy things. One day in ICU, I had been awake for a while, and I remember a giant brown wooden wardrobe falling right behind my dad. He remembers this day as I pointed at the wardrobe as if I had seen a ghost. He told me that he'll never forget the scared look I had on my face. Of course, he turned around and saw nothing. That same day I remember seeing two men at the back of the room, one with silver hair and the other blonde. I remember one wearing a leather jacket, and they were having their own conversation together and laughing. However, my dad claims that there was no one else in the room that day and remembers no one who looked like this coming to visit at all. It must have been some guys auditioning to be my Prince Charming already. Come on guys, I've only been awake for, like, two seconds! Another time I remember having trouble with the ventilator. I felt like it wasn't helping me breathe. I kept hallucinating strands of hair flying around the room and getting caught in my ventilator, choking me. I even remember when my cousin came to visit, she was sitting by my bed and I reached out to the hair that was floating around the room, which probably confused her. Everyone knew I was hallucinating so she must have wondered what I was trying to catch.

Although I was hallucinating a lot, my lungs were really weak. I was still struggling to breathe and I needed my ventilator. I remember trying to pull out the ventilator because it made me feel uncomfortable and I thought it was the reason I couldn't breathe. Breathing is such a natural thing that no one even thinks about, but when I couldn't even do that, it made me so uncomfortable. I couldn't understand why my parents were trying to hold me down, it made me so emotional because I couldn't speak to ask for help and I felt so frustrated that I wasn't able to move.

During my time in the ICU, I couldn't understand why I wasn't able to speak. No words were coming out of my mouth, as if I had lost my voice, like in "The Little Mermaid". I didn't understand what was happening to me. I tried many different ways to communicate. First, my dad held up a sheet with the alphabet, and I tried to have him spell out a sentence word by word. For some reason, this didn't work. I couldn't communicate, no one understood what I was trying to say.

I even tried to write things down. I began to write something, but the pen fell out of my hand. I was too weak to write on the paper. I just couldn't wrap my head around why I was so weak. I had a heated blanket on my bed, which I always begged them to turn up high. I would have it as high as 45 degrees Celsius, which still left me completely frozen!

At the time, I was doing speech therapy. But I have absolutely no memory of doing this. The only physiotherapy I remember doing in the intensive care ward was physical physiotherapy. It consisted of two physiotherapists trying to hold me up as I was too weak to hold myself up at the time. Sounds like my kind of exercise, someone else doing it for me.

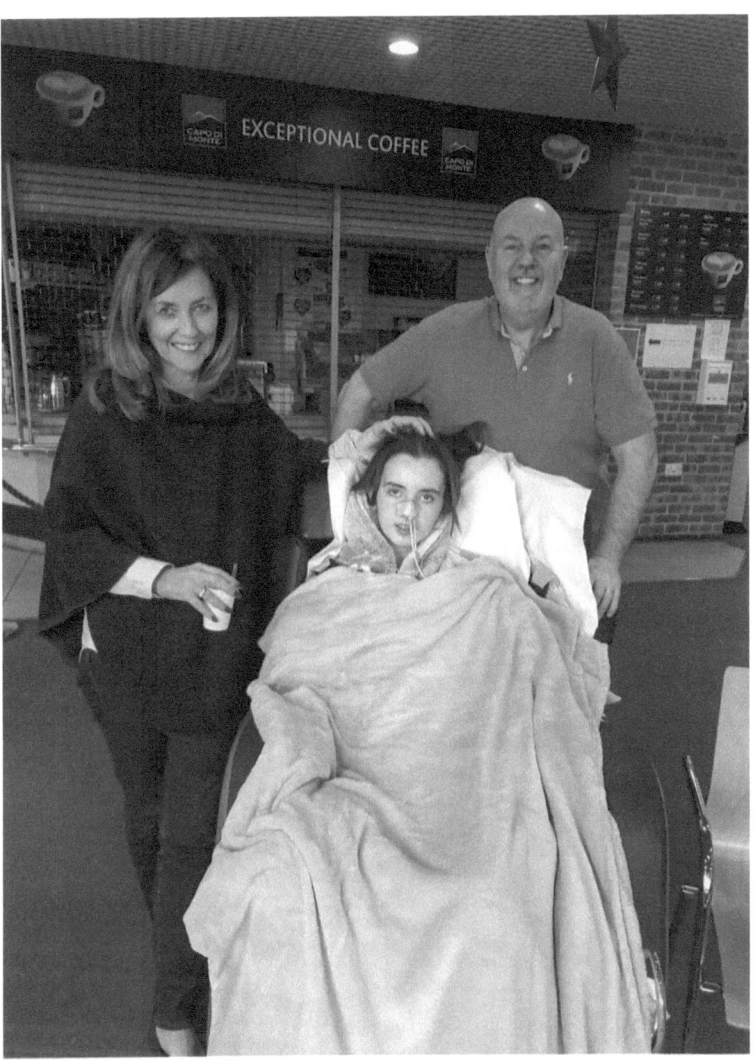

CHAPTER 3
RECOVERY

"Trying to find ways not to give up"

DECEMBER 2019

As I started to become more conscious, I started to become aware of my surroundings. My senses all came back individually, but not all at once. My vision was blurry as if I needed glasses, which was unusual as my eyesight wasn't bad before. I remember one eye being worse than the other. I couldn't hear anything when I first woke up, I remember my mum was playing one of my favourite tv shows on a laptop and I couldn't hear anything. I couldn't even hear them talk at first. I was so confused as to why I couldn't hear anything and why my vision was so blurry. What had happened to me? Although my hearing slowly started to come back within about a week, I was so heavily medicated that my mind was playing tricks on me. My mind made me believe that the hospital room was underwater. My hearing was muffled and my sight was unclear.

As my vision very slowly started to become clearer, I noticed some pictures on the wall. From my hospital bed, I wasn't able to see who was in the pictures. So, I made my dad take them off the wall so that I could see them. A few of my friends had sent pictures of us together, and my parents had put them up for me to see, and to make the room feel brighter. I also noticed a big whiteboard, which thankfully had letters big enough for me to read. It had a countdown to Christmas. It was CHRISTMAS?!? I couldn't believe how much time had passed. For me, it didn't even feel like a day. But I had missed most of November and December. The doctors stopped sedating me around the 20th of December which is when I remember officially opening my eyes. What a day to choose ... it was my mum's birthday! I don't really remember much from the first couple of days of waking up. I kept going in and out of consciousness.

Then it was Christmas, ...

25TH OF DECEMBER 2019

On Christmas Eve my whole family went out for Christmas dinner without me. I saw a family picture of them all on my phone. I really wished I was there with them, it's not often that we all got to spend Christmas together as we all live in different parts of the world. Of course, I felt sad as I was missing out on Christmas dinner with my family, which had never happened before, but I wanted them to have a little bit of a normal Christmas even if I couldn't. It wasn't so bad because I was tired anyway and really could use the rest.

I love Christmas so much. I tried so hard to stay awake the whole day, which was unusual for me at the time because I was always so tired and heavily medicated. However, since I couldn't be with my family, my favourite nurse tried to cheer me up by playing Christmas music while all of the nurses came into my room and they danced around. I tried my best to dance along with them although I couldn't move much. I couldn't even sit up. The best I could do was move my arms. Even though it could have been my worst Christmas, they made Christmas in the hospital not so awful. It was also probably hard for them to be working on Christmas Day, they likely wanted to be with their families, too. You know what? I'm sure it was nice for them to have someone like me who was a bit older in the kids' ward. Because the hospital I was in specialised in paediatric heart conditions, it was mostly babies in the kids' ward.

26TH OF DECEMBER 2019

Then Boxing Day came, the day after Christmas. As a kid, this was when I would spend the entire day playing with all the new toys that I got for Christmas. But for me it was awful. I remember being so sick that day because of how exhausted I was from the day before. I had tried so hard to stay awake for the whole day because I wanted to spend time with my family on Christmas. However, this wasn't normal for me at the time as I needed a lot of rest. But I'd say it was worth it because I managed to stay awake.

JANUARY 2020

Everyone was talking about COVID-19 but I didn't really think about it much. I was in my own world of suffering.

There I was, a couple of months since I'd woken up from a coma, and I couldn't even sit up in my hospital bed. It had been months! I thought that my illness was already over. I wasn't really feeling sick anymore. I had never experienced an illness like this or ever watched someone I knew go through it, so I didn't really know how long it would take me to recover. Normally if I was at home sick, it would take me a week or two to fully recover. What made this time so different?

I remember one of my nurses who frequently had to look after me, Dan, was my favourite nurse. I liked how he would treat me like a normal person, and not a sick patient in a hospital. Kind of like a friend, which is honestly something I really needed at the time. Especially at night when my mum would go back to her room to sleep, it was always so lonely, but Dan was always there to talk to. He would let me watch movies on his phone if I couldn't sleep. Which was often, because the pain would always wake me up. He would show me pictures of his pet parrot which he loved so much, and videos of him performing in a Christmas orchestra.

Dan was also the first nurse to let me eat something, which is pretty hard to forget. I think the first thing I ate was strawberry or peach yogurt. I couldn't even drink water. It was so hard to watch people drink in front of me. My body was too weak to drink it, it would make me sick. If water went down the wrong way and I started coughing, it would make me sick. I was so cautious with everything I did. For example, I held in my coughs. And when I eventually was allowed to have water, it would be from a sponge as I couldn't move much or do anything. Then I progressed to drinking from a spoon, and then finally from a straw.

It was times like these when I often thought of my grandad. Back in 2019 I never understood why or how he had changed so much. He would get angry at the littlest things and was easily irritated by someone or something. Every time someone would try to help him, he would become frustrated. I could never understand why. It's so different watching someone you love going through this to being in this position yourself. People often just want to help support you because you're sick but you still feel like the same person. On the outside, you may have changed but nothing about you has changed on the inside, so why has everyone else suddenly started treating you so differently? You haven't changed so why has everyone else? You also just don't want to accept the reality of it. You want to carry on with life as if it were still normal despite your physical health and you just wish that everyone would pretend along with you.

I never really understood what happens to us when we die, but a while after my grandfather passed, I saw him in my dreams. However, in my dreams he didn't look the way he did the last time I saw him. He looked the way I remembered him when I was growing up. I tried to talk to him in this dream but he just smiled at me in response. I'm glad he never had to see me like this. I had lost a lot of weight and was literally skin and bones. My face was pale, and I had feeding tubes in my nose. I was connected to many monitors. But I was happy that my hair was still healthy, and I am grateful to the nurses who were washing and brushing it regularly.

I remember the day that the nurse told me and my mum that the hardest part was going to be my recovery. He told us that it was going to take at least a year to recover. I didn't really believe him at first. At the time, I had no idea what he meant by this. What is recovery? Wasn't it already over? The thought of it confused me. My mum didn't know what to think, either. It was so shocking for me to hear. I thought I would just be able to get up one day and walk out. At this point I still didn't fully understand what had actually happened to me or the severity of it. I was quite literally a month behind everyone. When I woke up from the coma, it felt like only a few hours for me. I felt as if I had been on the school trip with my friends just the day before. I was, however, happy that I didn't have to go back to school to face that teacher that I hated.

I couldn't believe that I needed a physiotherapist to help me to do a simple task like sitting up without assistance, lifting my arms, or even turning my head from side to side. I was so lucky to have someone like my mum there every single day to help me eat and brush my teeth. I didn't understand why I was still so weak. I wasn't sick anymore and I was getting better. However, because I had been asleep for so long, my muscles had wasted away and, of course, I hadn't eaten anything so I weighed only 39 kg. In the past, building muscle had generally not been difficult for me, but when I didn't have any muscle at all, that made it more complicated.

I was so weak that I wasn't able to sit up in my hospital bed for months. Although the recovery was absolutely draining and painful, I'll admit that just sitting around watching movies all day was fun for a while. At least, it was fun until my classmates went back to school in January 2020, after the Christmas break. I honestly thought that I'd be going back to school with them. I don't really know why I thought this, I guess I just wanted it so badly. Which is weird because I honestly hated school. I only had one real friend that I would sit with at lunch, my other best friend having moved all the way back to Canada. I wouldn't have had it any other way though. One real friend is better than many not-so-great friends.

My best friend and I would get wraps for lunch together every day, and we sat next to each other in math class, failing miserably at trying to understand what was going on. On the days she wasn't there, I'd just sit alone. I don't know why someone would miss that, but those memories are so special to me now. I think the thing that made me feel the worst was the thought of her being the one that was alone. It's something I think I'll always feel guilty for. I know it was out of my hands but putting my friends through that is always hard for me to think about. There's nothing in this world I will ever regret more than leaving my best friend. Even if I thought it was only just going to be for a week, it is my biggest regret. My friends mean everything to me, and I hate thinking about what I put them through and how they felt when I was sick. At least I didn't really have to worry about my exams anymore, which I for sure would have failed.

FEBRUARY 2020

At some point in February 2020, I was transferred to a hospital in Scotland. My family was living there, so the transfer made it easier for them to be with me. I kept getting infections, so I had to stay in the hospital. Finally, I was able to leave on the 17th of April, which was earlier than the hospital would have liked, because I was still quite frail. It became too unsafe for me to be in there when the pandemic started. My lungs were still so weak that it would have been dangerous for me to catch COVID. Also, I quite literally begged my lead doctor to let me out, which somehow worked! I honestly didn't think it would, but I put up a very mean fight! When I got out, I thought I would feel a sense of victory but all I could think was, "thank God this part is finally over and I'm out". It's as if there had been a big rainstorm and the rain had finally stopped, but I was left with the aftermath of the destruction and floods. One problem was solved, but now I had to deal with the next one.

My mum and I stayed with my Gran which I liked because she cooked me breakfast every day, whatever I wanted. Her food was definitely better than the hospital food. Of course, I still strongly disliked the UK, but we made the best of a bad situation. We used the time to see family, as they all lived in Scotland. And my mum and I loved living with my granny, who made the UK not so bad, and I'm happy we could be there for her too as I know it hadn't been easy for her since my grandad passed away.

SEPTEMBER 2020

The summer passed with me still in recovery mode, during which I did and achieved absolutely nothing, and during which it was hard for me to get the care I needed because health workers were all focused on COVID patients. I still needed physiotherapy, which I only got once a week. During this time another school year began. It was not just any year but sixth form, the second last year of high school. Every single year of secondary school, all anyone talked about was the sixth form. It was kind of like the prize at the end of completing all those years of school, and I was missing it. All that hard work that I had done, and I wasn't even going to get to experience it. I kind of knew I wasn't going to be able to go back. I still couldn't walk, and I had made it clear to my parents that I would never go back in a wheelchair. If I was going to go back to school at all, then it would be by walking through the doors. At that time, medical expenses were going up, and my mum was struggling to get health insurance for me. It was harder and more expensive for me because I had been on an ECMO machine.

I didn't think everyone going back to school would affect me so deeply until I saw all the pictures and videos of everyone getting their new uniforms. I felt like I was missing out on the most important part of school life. I never thought I'd miss those days. It was just hard to watch everyone move on without me.

I felt as if people feeling sympathy for me was just a trend, and that people had already gotten bored of me. Eventually, their sympathy ran out and I was kind of forgotten about. It didn't help that I was feeling so isolated already by my physical disabilities. I couldn't walk, I was in a wheelchair and on medication. I would read, and chat with friends at times, but people were moving on with their lives. Of course, people still felt sorry for what happened to me, but not enough anymore to do anything about it or come and visit me.

I liked the sympathy at first. It had made me feel loved, until it stopped. I didn't want people to feel sorry for me. It made me despise any kind of sympathy that people gave me. Even today, I don't ever let someone speak to me in a patronising way. People who had called themselves my friends did things like throw parties and go out for dinners: things that they swore they would never want to do without me. It made me see more clearly who was truly there for me, and those people were my two best friends. They never needed me to be sick to care about me. They were the ones who were there for me since the beginning, who never needed a reason to be my friend. And, of course, there was my mum, who has looked after me my whole life.

Slowly I began to recover. I became physically stronger, which made it easier for me to not rely so much on the help of other people. However, after a while, my mum had to go back home to Dubai to work and take care of the house. This was so hard for me: I didn't know how I was going to live without her. It was really hard to see her go, but I remember staying strong because I know it was probably just as hard for her.

And, looking on the bright side, her leaving meant I was one step closer to going home.

I think being left in Scotland without my mum made me much more aggressive with the doctors. I was so jealous that my mum got to go home that it made me angry with every doctor I was seeing. I was angry that they didn't really care about me because I wasn't sick anymore. I just needed help physically. I had a wound on my leg for over a year because they couldn't figure out why it wasn't healing. But they never bothered to investigate further, they just left me to take care of myself. Eventually, I needed a skin graft, which is basically a skin transplant. They took a very thin layer of skin from my thigh and put it on the wound. Of course, when they did this, they discovered that the top layer of skin wasn't healing due to issues deeper in my leg.

I was so angry that it had taken them so long to figure this out. I knew they didn't care enough. I was just a job to them. I couldn't wait for the day when I would never have to see them again. I'm not generally an angry person but I had truly had enough. I needed one more operation before I was allowed to go home to Dubai. The doctor who lacked any bedside manner was treating me for this specific issue. I sarcastically named him Dr of *Happiness and Sunshine*. In reality, he was a miserable person. He refused to do the surgery because I had an open wound which is why I had the skin graft.

Once my skin had finally healed, he agreed to do the surgery. I also needed Achilles surgery on both of my Achilles' tendons because I had been in a hospital bed for so long that I had extremely bad drop-foot, which prevented me from walking. I couldn't move my feet; they were fixed in a pointed position. I hadn't known before that this was something that could happen. The nurses in London always put a bench at the bottom of my bed to keep my feet straight and prevent them from dropping. I had never really understood why. But once I got to Scotland, none of the nurses did a single thing to prevent my foot drop from getting so bad.

Although Doctor Sunshine had agreed to do the surgery, he had very bluntly told me that it probably wouldn't work. I know doctors aren't supposed to fill you with false hope and must tell you all the risks and what could go wrong, but did he have to be such an arrogant person? Both my mum and I despised this man's negativity, and she was never afraid of showing it. We both looked at each other after this man was done talking his nonsense as if we knew exactly what each other was thinking. Deep down I always just knew it would work. And it did. I had a strong intuition. I saw the miserable Dr Sunshine afterwards and he told me that he "didn't expect the surgery to go so well". It's not exactly what you want to hear from the man who just performed surgery on you. I looked at him with a blank face, because there was no point arguing or making a comment. Of course it would work! There was absolutely no reason for it not to be successful. He was just negative, and if I ever run into him again, I will definitely say this to his face because I wouldn't want to fill him with false hope. I would have to tell him the straight-up facts. I feel sorry for any patient that has to deal with him. Not everyone has a mum like mine to fight back against people like him who think they know everything when all they do is leave you with bad feelings and a headache.

I knew this would be the start of real recovery for me because it would mean that I could finally go home, and I would never have to rely on those doctors again. My health was in my hands. I would love to go back one day to see the looks on their faces when they see that I actually did it. Most of them never believed I would end up where I am today. It made me realise that even the "smartest" people in the world can be wrong. Yes, they have a higher education but I know what my body is capable of doing. These people don't even know me. I am just as smart as them, possibly even smarter. I was just a 16-year-old girl and I proved everyone in these hospitals wrong.

I discovered that you can only fail at something if you've given up. Giving up is not something that I was going to let happen. I had already gotten too far to give up. I finally was able to stand up and walk with crutches after months of being in a wheelchair. And to finally be able to move independently was a great feeling.

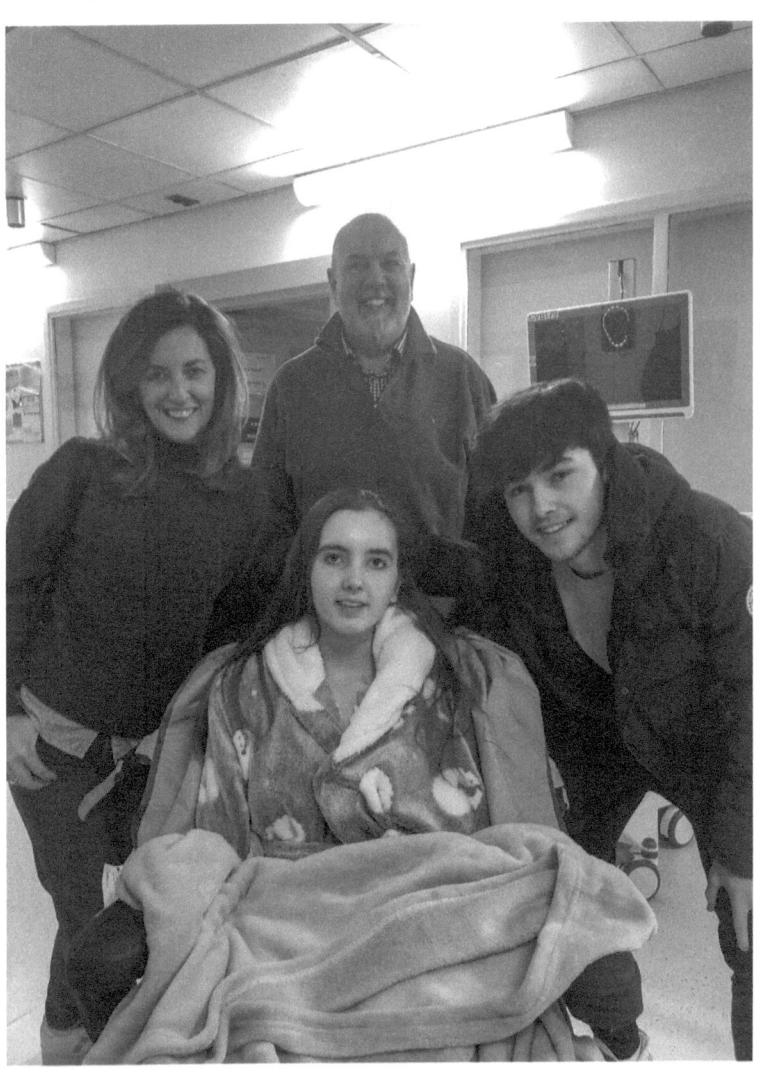

CHAPTER 4

GETTING BACK TO "NORMAL"

"Taking my life back"

5TH OF JUNE 2021

I did it! I was finally home in Dubai! Returning to my home in Dubai was something I almost gave up believing was possible for me but **I MADE IT**!

I was with my mum and my dog again, in my not-so-new house. It was still new to me because I hadn't lived in it for very long before I ran off to London. I couldn't contain my excitement on the plane, and I definitely couldn't sleep.

My plane landed around midnight. When I stepped off that plane, it felt as if I had never left Dubai. A few friends had come to meet me at the airport, but my flight had landed early, so I was the first person to arrive. I finally got to see my mum again. I went to bed that night feeling as if I had just had the worst nightmare ever. At this point, it had almost been 2 years since the accident. It was a moment in time when I could see the progress myself. But I still had a long way to go to recover physically. This was the moment I had been waiting for, for a very long time. All those nights in the hospital, wishing I could be home in my own bed. When I woke up the next morning, I got up and just stared out my bedroom window. It was a sight for sore eyes. I was home!

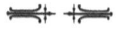

JUNE 2021

Before school started, I had some trouble getting the school to allow me to join year 13 with my friends. They told me I had missed too much school, and that it wouldn't be possible for me. Of course, me being the stubborn person that I am, I refused. I had fought too hard to be there and it made me feel so angry because I know none of this was my fault, it was out of my hands. At first, I just accepted it, I wasn't going to go back to that school if it wasn't on my terms.

I wasn't alone in this fight. My mum fought for me and had many meetings with the school, and she has never liked hearing the word "no". Originally, I had picked the AS subjects English Language and Media, but I had decided that those subjects just weren't for me. I met with the performing arts department, and they agreed to let me take the music B-tech degree. But instead of me doing this course for 2 years, they allowed me to complete it in 1 year and were so helpful in creating a schedule for me. I also spoke to my best friend India and asked for her advice. She suggested I do a Geography AS, which is half an A level so it would only take 1 year. She assured me that if I chose geography, she would help me with it and her mum would as well. I'm really grateful for India and for her mum, as well as for the entire performing arts department.

I definitely couldn't have done it without them. Although geography was the main reason I had wanted to go to London in the first place, it didn't mean it couldn't be the reason I could graduate.

GETTING BACK TO "NORMAL"

SEPTEMBER 2021

When I went back to school, it was a very bittersweet moment. Words couldn't even describe how happy I was. It was something I had waited a year and a half for and I couldn't believe it was finally happening. Life finally started to feel a little bit normal again. However, on the other hand, I was terrified. I was the new girl suddenly, except almost everyone knew who I was and knew what had happened to me. I was the only new person in year 13, and I was on crutches. I was scared of people staring at me or, even worse, asking me about it. I hated talking about it and still do. I fear that's all people think when they look at me. Even the principal told me at the end of the school year that he felt scared for me. He always invited me to his office to talk, it made me not feel so alone. I wasn't really stable on my feet at this point. I couldn't believe I was finally able to go back to school, it almost made the fight feel worth it.

Honestly, I had been terrified about going back to school. I felt as if I would be the odd one out, not just physically, but mentally too. All my classmates had had an extra year to decide their futures, what they wanted to do, and where they were going. But for me, I felt as if I'd had no time to decide. All my friends were applying to universities, and I wasn't. Not only was it the last thing I wanted to do, but my life had become so unpredictable: I had no idea what life would look like for me a month from now, never mind a year. I had also just gotten back to Dubai and I wasn't ready to say goodbye just yet. I hate that there's so much pressure on young people to pursue higher education, and if they don't, they are perceived as failures. There are always other options.

I met a new girl, Hannan, though, and from the first moment we hung out we became best friends. She was new to the school the previous year and had no idea who I was or what had happened to me. She made my last year in high school not suck so much, and I am very grateful for her and her sister. We're inseparable: wherever she goes, I go.

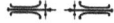

APRIL 2022

My mum messaged me one day asking if I wanted to go to a festival with her friend in California. She said the festival was called "Coachella" and, of course, I said yes because who would ever say no? I was a bit excessive and planned an outfit for every day and even brought spare clothes just in case, I was so excited. I had never been to California but it had always been a dream of mine. We visited so many cool places in Los Angeles before driving to Palm Springs for the festival. I was so nervous to be at this festival because LA is so intimidating. I was thinking to myself, "Who am I compared to these LA girls? They're probably all so beautiful and have the most amazing outfits". But when I was there, that thought never even crossed my mind. It was literally like something out of a movie, with so many celebrities walking past left and right. And I got to meet some of my favourite people ever. I had been so worried about the way other people would see me that I didn't even imagine how much fun I was going to have. Not to mention some of the best artists and bands ever were performing. When I got back to school everyone was talking about me, in a good way. I was the cool girl that went to LA, not the girl that was in a coma. I'm glad I changed my image in school.

JUNE 2022

I finally graduated high school. Graduation ceremonies are quite American, but we had one anyway. They split the year group into two because the school was so big and there were just too many of us for one ceremony. My ceremony was the first one which was SO early in the morning. I had to wake up at 6 am to do my makeup and get ready. I really enjoyed it though, there were performances and speeches and each student went up to get their certificate, one by one.

I needed help to get on the stage as there were a lot of steps. I was a bit embarrassed because no one else had needed help. Then my name was called, and I walked forward to shake the Head Teacher's hand and receive my certificate but suddenly there was a loud cheer in the room. After each name was called everyone had clapped but when my name was called there was a loud cheer. I wasn't expecting it but it made me so happy to know that everyone else was aware of the progress I had made, like they had been cheering me on from afar. Or maybe they just felt bad that I couldn't get up and down the stairs without needing someone to help me.

After the graduation ceremonies were over, everyone got all dressed up for prom. I went a little crazy and got my hair and makeup professionally done, but, hey, you only have one prom, right? I wore a long black silky dress that I'd had made. A few of my friends came over before and we ate some food before going to prom in a limo. Prom was a bit boring, to be honest, but the parties afterwards were where the fun was. I knew that this would be the last time I would see most of these people so I tried to enjoy the moment.

CHAPTER 5

WHEN WILL IT BE OVER?

"Is there a light at the end of the tunnel?"

JUNE 2022

It's been three years now and my recovery is still causing me problems. Every time I think it's over, something new happens and I'm faced with a new obstacle. Here I am with another infection. Life has been so chaotic for three years: all I want is for things to be normal again. I want to be able to do everyday tasks without needing someone else's help. I miss living with my mum in our old house and getting coffee together with her, going to the movies, and her not having to worry about me as much as she does. I miss playing with my dog on the beach. I miss the freedom of walking along the beach by myself and feeling the sand under my feet. Never in a million years did I think I would miss something as simple as a touch sensation. But it's something that haunts me every day.

I miss not having physical limitations and not knowing what the inside of a hospital looks like, because I'm there almost every day now. I miss not having my insecurities limit what I wear Before, I would just throw anything on and not think anything of it, but now I find myself wearing clothes to cover up my scars. I miss when things were simpler, living with mum in the old house, taking my dog to the beach and letting her swim around in the ocean. I know I'll never be the same person I used to be, which makes me sad.

Every day when I look in the mirror, I am reminded it is not possible for me to be the person I was before. I can't change the way I look, and I certainly can't erase my memories.

Every time I meet new people and make new friends, I always wonder what they would have thought of me if they had met me back in 2019 when I was just a normal 15-year-old girl. I wasn't perfect, of course: I was extremely shy and had no confidence at all. I had no idea what I wanted to do, but I couldn't even think about that because I was so worried about passing my GCSEs that I didn't think about the future. It didn't help that I was failing a lot of classes and wasn't mentally strong enough to fix that.

It makes me sad that my current reality is what people's perception of me is. I'm the girl who was in the wrong place at the wrong time because I went on a school trip to London. I don't want to be known for being in an accident, I want to be a normal girl. Growing up you often want to stand out and be different, but once you do there's no way you can go back to being normal. I can't even go out wearing shorts anymore for fear that people will stare at me. I always feel more comfortable covering up, to help me blend in. It's one of the rare moments when my mind is at peace. I can't believe that after everything, my self-confidence has been completely destroyed. I buy all these pretty dresses and skirts, but I still don't have the courage to wear them out in public. I'm not necessarily worried about what people will think of me, but when they stare at me and ask me what happened to my legs, it really changes my entire mood and makes me feel so embarrassed and just different from everyone else.

I don't want to complain too much. I mean from a different point of view, they all look like first-world problems. These things don't really matter in the end. Life is all about perspective, because there are so many things that the newer version of me has that the old version didn't. For instance, happiness. Although I'm still battling many issues in life, I've never been happier. I'm surrounded by the most amazing people. Even though I have to carry some of the worst memories with me for the rest of my life, I know that there are so many great memories for me to make in the future.

I could sit around feeling sorry for myself over things that I can't change, or I could use it to be better. For example, a hero and a villain can have the same life story, but the villain uses their past as an excuse to feel sorry for themselves and the hero uses it to make things better and to help other people. I know sometimes I fall down this spiral of feeling sorry for myself, but I want to be the hero. I want to help other people. Life isn't fair, it never has been and it probably never will be. You'll never truly appreciate something until you don't have it anymore. And if I'm not aware of the fact that life isn't fair, there are many people who will remind me. Sometimes people say, "Everything happens for a reason". I have never hated a sentence more in my life. No one deserves the bad things that life gives them, there isn't a reason for the pain. And, sure, there are "people who have it worse" than I do, but everyone's feelings and emotions are valid. I shouldn't have to feel guilty for wanting to get better. I deserve everything that every "normal" person has, and I won't settle for less.

People always tell me how strong I am. You may be thinking this about me right now, but I don't feel it most of the time.

I only look strong because I got through it, but to me, there was no other option. I knew I didn't deserve what happened to me, no one deserved that. Terrible things happen to people sometimes but you'll know it's in the past when it just feels as if it's a part of your life story. I knew I would make it through because I wasn't going to accept anything less. I always had this feeling right from the beginning that I was going to get through it. I was going to go home and live the life that I had always wanted to live. I was going to go home and take control because I was so tired of people telling me what I could and couldn't do.

4TH OF NOVEMBER 2022, DUBAI

The vascular surgeon wants to remove the catheter from my leg. It has stopped most of the blood flow in my leg which has caused so many different infections. The catheter was left in my artery when they were trying to connect me to the ECMO machine. The surgeon told me that it wasn't harming my body at the time but it could block my blood flow at any moment. You can't have foreign bodies inside you at all. It's obviously not natural and you can't live like that forever. We have no idea what damage this catheter in my artery has or has not caused. This has obviously never happened before.

This was also the day my doctor put me under a general anaesthetic so he could put a tube through my leg to clean out the staphylococcus aureus infection.

5TH OF DECEMBER 2022

After three years, on the day I finally had the catheter removed from my groin, the doctor told me that it had completely destroyed my artery and that they had to do a bypass. It was a very scary procedure for me as it was obviously not done often, and I find it very hard to trust any doctor these days after everything that happened with previous doctors like my good friend Dr Sunshine. However, I am very happy with my current doctor and I trusted him completely to save me.

The surgery took five hours to complete. It was the most painful surgery I've ever had to recover from. He had to cut through my stomach muscles and stitch them back up, so doing absolutely anything involving using those muscles was complete agony, like coughing or sneezing or even laughing! Which is a shame because I think I'm quite the comedian and even laugh at my own jokes. But it's crazy how much my blood flow has changed since the operation. It was immediately better when the catheter was removed. My legs were warm again! Hopefully, this means I can grow back some muscles, which I have been failing miserably at doing. I also feel nerve pain from time to time which I think means that my nerves are finally growing back. I do have more sensation already, which makes me so happy you have no idea! I'll be running along the beach in no time!

22ND OF DECEMBER 2022

I hadn't gotten rid of the infection in my leg so they attached a small machine to my leg which washed out the wound. The machine was so loud and made a noise every 30 seconds! I took it out on Christmas Day so I could have a normal day, but this might have been a mistake. It made my leg worse but to be honest I don't regret it. I had an amazing Christmas with my boyfriend who I met when I went back to school last year, and I wouldn't have changed a thing.

14TH OF JANUARY 2023, DUBAI

My doctor thought it would be best for me to have another surgery to completely open up my leg and clear out the leftover infection. I just wanted it to be over so, of course, I agreed. It wasn't easy for me to agree to another surgery, but this was a doctor I trusted completely. I had a big machine attached for the first couple of days, which washed out the wound. It was heavy, though, and was the size of a computer, so it was like a workout every time I got up to use the bathroom. However, then I got a smaller machine. They're only programmed to last 7 days, so every week we have to buy a completely new machine because they keep dying. They are programmed to die, so you have to buy a new one. It seems very strange to have such marketing for hospital equipment, but who am I to judge, I guess. After three weeks, they finally removed the machines and let my leg heal on its own. At last I feel like I'm winning in this spiralling game I seem to be playing! I can finally go back to the gym, which I have grown to love since recovery.

To be honest, I don't think there's an answer to the question, "When will it be over?". I think life will keep throwing obstacles at me until the very end. This may be my life forever, or it may not. I can't see into the future or change the past. I can only work on the things I can change.

And I'm grateful for what I have achieved. I remember when I wished for days like this. I have so much independence now, and I don't need anyone's assistance. I can go for a walk around the park on my own or go to a coffee shop. I get to experience life the way everyone else does. I've made new friends, and fallen in love, and all these new people in my life have decided that this version of me is worth knowing and keeping around. Maybe they think that this version of me is even better. I have control. One day this whole experience will be so far in the past, that I might even forget about it … sometimes.

NOTES

www.ingramcontent.com/pod-product-compliance
Lightning Source LLC
Chambersburg PA
CBHW021121080526
44587CB00010B/597